TACKING LESSONS

Poems by
Nancy Bailey Miller

TACKING LESSONS
Poems by Nancy Bailey Miller

Published by
The Cheshire Press
A Division of The Cheshire Group, Inc.
PO Box 2090
Andover, Massachusetts 01810
www.cheshirepress.com

ISBN: 978-0-9821924-3-6
Library of Congress Control Number: 2016944566

Printed in the United States of America

Cover design: Nancy Parsons
Photo credit: Leighton O'Connor
Back cover photo: Don Miller

Fermata Books
6 Ashwood Drive
North Reading, MA 01864
nancybaileymiller@gmail.com

THE
CHESHIRE
PRESS

For Don,
my husband and partner of fifty years
who taught me to tack in his fifteen foot sailboat,
Bedlam, when we were in junior high.
From Manhasset Bay to Marblehead Harbor,
from Tortola to Anegada,
whether anchored at Misery Island
or heeling in half a gale near Cane Garden Bay
we learned from the ocean, the boat, the wind.

By the Author

Dance Me Along the Path

Of Minitemen & Molly's

Before the Dove Returns: A Gallery of Portrait Poems

Making Strawberry Pies and Other Ways We Become Grandmas

Risking Rallentando

Hold On

The following poems have been previously published:

"Beach Plum Jelly," *Poetry Porch* online, Spring 2016, Joyce Wilson, editor

"Obituary," *Lighten Up Online*, June 6, 2016, Jerome Betts, editor

"Salt Water and Fresh," *Walk With Me*, March 2016, South Church, Andover, Massachusetts

"On Reading Robert Wrigley's 16 Tips, Quips & Pontifications the Week after my 50th Reunion," *Poem of the Moment*, masspoetry.org website, July 6, 2015, Jacquelyn Malone, editor

"Time to Reboot," *The Poetry Porch: Sonnet Scroll*, Joyce Wilson, editor, www.poetryporch.com, Summer 2009

"Cairn," *Power of Prayer*, April 2013, South Church, Andover, Massachusetts

"Taking Chances," *Hold On*, Nancy Bailey Miller, Fermata Press, 2012

"Time to Reboot," *Hold On*, Nancy Bailey Miller, Fermata Press, 2012

CONTENTS

Taking Chances   11

Test Me   12

Beach Plum Jelly   13

Raw Water and Fresh   15

Tacking Lessons   16

Status   17

Eerste Helmersstaat   18

Zip Line in Chile With Strangers   19

Rubén's Story   20

Outside The Textile Shop   22

Wrong Direction   24

Why Jack Ewing Got into Eco-tourism   26

Watching Scarlet Macaws   27

My Destiny   28

I have been thinking   29

Cairn   30

Flight 370   31

Contrail   32

Conversation at the Furniture Restoration Shop   33

Face to Face   36

Munsey Park   37

Melt   38

Epiphany   39

Truth Be Told   40

Dressing Up   41

Testifying   42

Honestly?   43

After Election Day, 2012   44

Vengeance, Saith The Crowd   45

Time To Reboot   46

Obituary   47

Pearl Street On Saturday Night   49

Trail Head   50

Eavesdropping at my 50th Reunion   51

On Reading Wrigley's 16 Tips   52

Notes   56

Ashes   59

The Poems

Taking Chances

Just take the plunge. Leap from the boat
though you wear glasses, shoes and phone.
It's not a crisis—swim or float,
just take the plunge! Leap from that boat.
The other shore may be remote
yet worth the effort. Grouse or groan
but take the plunge. Leap from the boat—
you can replace your shoes and phone . . .

Test Me

Ocean, I am your daughter. Seaweed in my hair,
I am married to the deep—Neptune's girl,
seduced by salty biceps, I drink your inky eyes.
With the bait of your singing, I swim to your pull.

Fill my snorkel with sea salt. Blind me
with your murkiness. Slash and dash me
on black volcanic rock. Vex and toss me
on your lumpy sheet, its lacy foam.

Send your sharks—with young sea lions
to school me, I'll flip from fish jaws. Send
ten orcas! Green turtles will cry them all calm.
You, my perilous playmate, *you* will not

swallow me. I'll wash the salt from my eyes,
cleanse my wounds in freshwater.
I'll return to you frolicking, flirting—
but, ocean, you'll not be my grave.

Beach Plum Jelly

I.
For Mother, it's an early start.
Break of day we cross to Palmer's Cove,
while low tide laps the sandbar.

Basket picnic, folding chair, red Thermos,
each of us with a blue tin bucket. Today
Mother doesn't tell my sister she is fat.

Coppertone slathered over our bodies,
white tees cover our bathing suits, our shoulders,
protect our fair and freckled skin.

Early plovers have not landed here to sample,
but the plums are ripe. We fill our pails—
ample to pick before the tide turns.

At noon we're wading to our knees;
we cross to lunch set on the army blanket.
No talk of Father's faults, today.

II.
In the kitchen Mother ties the quarts
of purple fruit in double cheesecloth,
fills the white enamel pot with water.

While we are banished, berries bubble, simmer
on the stove. All day she sterilizes Mason jars—
her cousin died from botulism on the farm.

Her double boiler melts the blocks of wax.
By dinnertime the pectin, sugar,
beach plum juice are in the jars,

the wax poured, soft and setting.
Tonight, she'll tighten down the tops.
From some things she protects us.

Raw Water and Fresh
two triolets

I.
Saltwater—raw, untreated—flushes out
the engine, also heads on boats. And tears
are like that too: they flush the sadness, doubt.
Raw water, salt depleted, flushes out
the sludge—embarrassments, regrets, and fears.
I dread raw water, raw emotion flushing
me, but free, released, it's merely tears.

II.
Freshwater on a boat is precious stuff.
Drink it like friendship—savor every sip.
If deep, a dialogue has just enough
freshwater in reserve—it's precious stuff—
to calm the oceans of our fears and grip
a shoulder's ache. It's precious stuff.
With you, my friends, I savor every sip.

Tacking Lessons

To change your course on sailboats you can tack,
"go through the wind," to go the other way.
Practice on the sea—you'll get the knack.

Speed comes from heading off. You must not lack
the control speed gives to change direction. Stay
one course—you might hit rocks—so tack

away. Reverse your life at dead ends. Pack
when some disaster spoils your holiday.
Practice change on land—you'll get the knack.

If you don't act with speed you might turn back.
Confronting power or abuse could sway
resolve to change your course for good. So tack!

Listen to calm voices on your track.
At any age the role of protégé
can help you practice till you get the knack.

To find my own direction I'll go smack
into the wind, not fear the disarray.
When changing course in life we have to tack.
I'll practice with my peers—we'll get the knack.

Status

Welcome all passengers, Flight 82,
the microphone crackles; I've arrived at the gate.
Two stretches of carpet one red and one blue

divided by stanchions. The edgy move near,
as jetway doors open; folks pack up their snacks.
Execs tune to Blackberries plugged in each ear.

First: Star Gold and Gold Elite, Silver Star holders,
a summons for servicemen dressed in fatigues. Next,
parents with lattes, kids texting in strollers.

You might expect Chase Card Explorers in minks.
All special-needs persons, step up on the double!
Plush lounges, express lanes, more legroom, "free" drinks:

such perks for the journey are actually faux—
they convince us we're privileged in sweatpants and fleece.
Now boarding zone five. At last I can go.

"We must be the losers," I suddenly sigh.
The one other person in zone five replies,
"At least we are boarding—not like that stand-by."

Eerste Helmersstraat

Amsterdam

Outside, a rolling suitcase on the sidewalk
like clip-clop hooves, like *die klompen* wooden shoes.
I open the drapes to early filtering sun,
rustle of beech trees, cooing pigeons.
Stone benches in the park across the one-way *straat.*
Rusted racks of nestled box bikes, creaking wagon bikes
with chinging bells; bar bikes off to work
on whirring wheels in brick bike lanes.

Yesterday I bought a ticket, took a chance
with "Hop-on-Hop-off" near the Leideseplein.

Pink hydrangea, yellow roses, purple hollyhocks.
Peaks of tall and snuggled houses:
bell shapes, step shapes, hooks on every roof
to pully chairs and beds to upper floors.
Curving bridges, narrow sidewalks,
striped awnings over storefront produce,
buttery smell of croissants baking,
magnetic pull of *koffie* brewing.

Zip Line in Chile with Strangers

Shoulders shivering, mouth dry,
we cross bridges to platforms,
not enough layers of Polartec.
I'm hooked twice to the cables,
metal clip on my belt for the zip.

Ninety meters above *Río Fuy*,
level with leafy tops of *el bosque*.
Will the wire hold? Will my clip?
My hands and knees shake,
instructions are not in my language.

¿Entiende usted? Do I?
*Cross feet. Don't brake early,
Use the leather-palmed glove.*
¿Lista? Ready? whispers the guide.
¡Me voy! The release! I am screaming—

the race of the canopy trees,
pine branches slapping my cheek,
birds screech, crescendo of cable vibration.
Nearby volcano ash spewing,
I am high as the condor, I am wings!

Rubén's Story

In our jungle village,
where máma taught third grade,
the Mormon church had built
a huge stone building,
fancy soccer fields to walk past
on our way to grade school.
Mormon missionaries visit
Máma every week or so.
"No, sorry, we're *católicos*."

My little brother Juan and I are
home alone one day.
Mormons knock again.
"What do we have to do
to join your church?"
(and use your soccer fields . . .)

"Be baptized in a pool? That's it?
Come back next week—
we'll talk to Máma!"

"Máma, Mormons have *piscina!*"
Picture laps, no dirty rivers filled
with snakes and bugs.
We imagine diving boards,
both high and low, Olympics
in our future. "Máma, yes, we *really*
want to join their church!"

The day we join *¡Que lástima!*
In the church a tiny pool—
no swimming lanes, no diving board—
this pool no bigger than a coffin.
Next week Mormons come again
to see our máma. A tithe
is due them—ten percent
of all she has.
We have to quit the church.

Outside the Textile Shop
Chinchero, Peru

"See those two clay bulls
on every roof?" asks Rubén.
"When couples marry, women
tie their braids together.
Grandpas, uncles hoist small bulls.
Good luck for making *ninos.*"

As yellow petals shower round our heads,
three beaming weavers bob a welcome.
These *señoras* spinning llama wool
on wooden spindles, wearing
woven skirts, embroidered blouses.
Black sombreros cover raven braids.

Near the wall, and to one side,
a bent, brown shape against the stone.
Wizened, wrinkled, now she shuffles
closer. Tattered shoes, a ragged shawl,
braids undone, a widow.
Our group sidesteps her gaze.

Rubén interrupts himself—
"Máma línda, buenas días."
Small coins jingle from his pocket
to her furrowed hand.
She squinks her toothless smile,
then hobbles down the cobbled street.

Wrong Direction

I have directions for the route.
My riding partner sick,
I ride today alone. I best leave first,
the others faster than Diana, Mercury,
faster than the Tour de France.
Ride Death Valley! shout their tight redblack bike shirts.
The website said this tour was easy. Right?

My palms sweat in my neon bike gloves.
I take off—like a shot—
parking entrance, stone wall
up to the right does not seem right
now I am Alice. Which card to pick?
Down to the left, I'm guessing,
yes, Pueblo Bisbal's surely down
so then to the left I'm flying
close to the edge, wind whistles
eyes burn, I whip sharp turns—
it's the foot of the hill that stops
me: one way a bridge, the other dirt.
This is not right.

At this fork, an artist at his easel,
sketching Dali's castle, medieval.
In the distance, Pyrenees capped with snow.
I breathlessly inquire:
El pueblo de Bisbal? Donde está?
His kindly Brit response:
Quite easy: back up this hill
past that large hotel castle—
then
over and down—
straight away to the village.

My tour will be gone.
Not right at all.
I'm left.

Why Jack Ewing Got into Eco-tourism

"Moved from Colorado in the sixties
after working just a few months for my dad.
Three guys from Nashville had me transport
thirty head of Colorado cattle on a DC-6.

"Idea was to keep them healthy five months
for new Costa Rican owners.
Later brought the wife, the kids.
Stayed here forty years.

"Men here hunted *pakas*
huge, fruit-eating rats—the meat is sweet.
Of course I had a gun in Colorado—
Always went deer hunting with my dad.

"One night a worker treed and shot . . . an ocelot.
I stroked her auburn, black-striped fur,
and looked into her sorrel eyes—
changed my heart."

Watching Scarlet Macaws
Punta Leona, Costa Rica

On the Tárcoles River—
in a far off kapok tree, a pair.

I'd love a longer, closer look. At noon
they'll fly to Playa Blanca for the almonds.

Drifting in Pacific waves,
I hear them argue, flapping, scrapping.

At sunset, from a low palm branch at pool's rim,
this macaw pair studies me, so still.

Both sexes scarlet, raucous,
partnered here for life. Raising hell

and chicks each year for fifty seasons.
What's their secret?

My Destiny

I am the queen of the leaf-cutter ants:
Pampered, fed, groomed, by my specialized staff
in my underground palace of tunnels and banquets.
Day and night, thousands of daughter ants scurry out—
hurry back, carrying snippets of citrus leaves,
back to our underground gardens of fungus,
the food of my colony—eight million ants—
feeding the farmer ants, soldier ants, me.

I lay a queen egg once every year,
a princess with wings who will start her own lair.
She flies, precious fungus stashed in her mouth—
mates in the air. Not so easy to pair with so many—
I remember how hard to hold two billion
fertilized eggs. My child queen creates a new colony
far far away. She lays eggs, soon her personal slaves.
When they grow as I did—she ingests her own wings.

I have been thinking

about loneliness and solitude:
loneliness ringing in ear canals
no milk in the refrigerator
even the cat has wandered off
loneliness buys a rat-a-tat ticket
on an empty train hurtling to Helvorgotten
fearing the bone black end

solitude whispers "Cassiopeia"
though a raven circles the cobalt sky
pine tops whistle a wandering spring
while claret embers simplify
a short story told
on an empty porch swing
near a pond without ripple

Cairn

Prayers piled in a stack
of round flat stones:
gathered in Sedona,
balanced, rough-brushed
against torrents, each oblation
a plate offering oxblood, henna.
Stones leached of pretense
infused with story,
the foe of speed.

Prayers stacked on our hearts
under a lapis sky.
Time collects them on the mesa,
breaks and rounds them,
shapes us all.
Below, the arroyo,
mere dust of dried steer's blood,
offers them.
Curious, the grace with which we
treasure our disappointments.
Is this how
to balance loss?

Flight 370

Not brass, nor stone, nor earth, nor boundless sea...
William Shakespeare, *Sonnet #65*

Fifty cabin snacks and forty meals uneaten.
Snoring business suits. Empty plastic goblets.
Sleeping children. Cell phones in the off position.
Earbuds whispering white noise to an ocean hush.

From fifteen countries Search and Rescue delves
between the surface and the mountain range of watery stone
three miles below the diatoms and sharks.
A soundless sea.

Breaking news spins out from towers—
days and nights and days
unbroken no news trace of nothing.
Drones—no bones, no wings. No knowing.

Contrail

As the engines' *whirr*
lifts me on silver wings
high above the Peace River,

I wish for a day without
the memory of Dad's death.
I hear the hum of him

trimming his purple hibiscus,
raking sea-grape leaves, belly flopping
into his pool to huff and splash laps.

Impish eyes behind thick horn-rims,
he'd tease us, he'd pun. His tattered blue
guidebook of birds, black binoculars trained

on a white egret stalking fish
in the culvert, the flight of an ibis,
a blue heron just after takeoff.

Conversation at the Furniture Restoration Shop

Harlan Moulton's shop, a gutted cape on Windsor Street off Main.
He's just completed sanding twenty pieces: Chippendale credenza,
Chinese chiffonier, inlaid armoire, maple drop-leaf table,
matching chairs. My white shorts are blackened with dust.

"It was my father's dresser after Mother Marie passed on.
Held Daddy's bow ties, undershirts, plaid skivvies,
starched white shirts secured with paper tapes.
Remember those? On top a leather box with cufflinks;
a milk glass ship held pennies, dimes. (I stole some once.)"
Harlan raises just one bushy eyebrow.

"Would they have bought this piece in Cincinnati?"

> "No, for sure it's handmade: 1840s, '50s.
> Greek Revival, more than likely crafted
> by a cabinetmaker up in Chillocothe.
> Your great-granddad might have paid
> a year of vegetables or maybe wheat."

"I'd like the wood a little lighter; could the cigarette burn come off?"

"No problem with the burn, but lighter?
This, my dear, is cherry; you can't make it into oak!
I'll always do the bidding of my customer... but
for the love of god, please don't put oak on cherry!
Here, let me show how cherry stain enriches,
brings out all the grain, removes the scratches.
Yikes! Don't touch it! Now you'll need
to wipe your finger on my rag."

"How will you fix the crack here on the top?"

"No way that we fix that! First of all," he sighs,
"the filler'd never stay. In ten or twenty years
it'd buckle up and just look bad. The crack adds character.
It's not veneer to patch. It's solid cherry.
How big's the tree trunk of a cherry?
Right. Your hands could almost reach around it.

"Now, look smart. How wide are these boards
on top? That's right. A good foot—
thirteen inches. These were 'first cut' cherry,
growing from the start of time. Maybe old as Eve.
No, we won't touch that crack."

In the van, he brought a wheezing, white-haired gent,
red bandana tied around his sweating forehead,
grunting the finished dresser up a flight.

> "Save this bureau scratched and water-stained
> from thirty years in basement exile? Some
> would not have paid the price."

A family mirror now hangs right above. I see
my father's blue eyes twinkling with delight.

Face to Face

From Grandmother's Waverly farm
I've inherited the antique mirror.
I witness: a flat-chested girl,
with my dimple, my curls.

She loathes her image, has cut
her arm, harbored more menacing
measures. In her dreams, she runs
from black wolves with bared teeth.

I tell her:
Before you do the dishes,
paint your nails cha-cha coral.
Buy toucan-green socks.

I tell her:
Go to the movies at noon.
Play Mozart quartets.
Be a good mother to yourself.

I tell her:
Your children will swirl
in dreams without wolves.

Munsey Park

I rode my blue, fat-tired bike on Ryder Road,
on Homer Place, on Whistler. All the streets
in Munsey Park were named for American
painters. Mr. Munsey set the rules:
slate roofs, colonial doors.

We lived on Remington. "Frederic,"
Mother loved to call it. Johnny lived
on Hunt Lane. Mother liked his family,
but he had such sweaty palms—
I knew from ballroom dance on Fridays.

Miss Wheeler and her husband, Mr. Bob,
taught sixth-grade dancing in the gym. I
attended Wheeler Ballet School on Mondays.
No women kept their maiden names,
but Mother said Miss Wheeler *did*
because she was an artist, a Professional.

A square dance in the gym on Halloween.
I, a mermaid: sequins, ribbons,
sea-foam tapered to my ankles,
a creation of my mother's Singer.
Mother called the black and gold
machine a *Sargent*—with a wink.
No one but our family got it.

Melt

The thing is
you may bitch
about removing me   but

you may also love the way
I slow you down
lend seconds minutes

hours to tidy up
those wine corks and elastics
in the kitchen drawer

time to simmer lentil soup
to call an ailing friend in Lakeland.

Hushed by blue of clearing sky and
lengthening pine tree shadows

a flame of cardinal flashes
against my white.

Dear texting tourist
on this spinning globe

in only moments I am cleared
I seep
I melt away

           Sincerely,
           Snow

Epiphany
Feast of Three Kings, January 6

Last Sunday, wise children
garbed in ruby robes
glittered Kmart crowns

passed bowls of golden stars.
Under each paper star one word—
In turn we each chose ours.

One child-king ascended to the choir loft.
A few stars in her basket.
I looked, I made my choice, I took my star, then

turned it over:
TRUTH.
Damn, I thought, damn.

I want
GIVING
RENEWAL
FORGIVENESS
KINDNESS

but my star says
TRUTH.

Truth Be Told

We seldom see the naked truth.
She changes clothes throughout her drama:
Mikado kimono or pinstriped suit.

In carmen chiffon, she might feather her eyes
with a green and gold mask from Mardi Gras.
A taut bustiér to enhance décolleté.

On script at center stage, or prompter
in the wings, she loves both trap door
and spotlight. Sometimes a troubadour

framed by dark velvet curtains, shimmery scrim.
Deep bow to applause, she exits left.
"Get to the bottom of yourself, Miss Truth.

"Come clean, and tell us all you've got!"
"No way. *Pas du tout!* Today I speak French,
tomorrow Russian. I'm a polyglot."

Dressing Up

Miss Truth installs a three-way mirror
when she comes to my boudoir.
Ceiling to floor, she tells me
if my slip needs hitching or
a sweater stitch is snagged—
she knows how quickly things unravel,

knows how hard I try
to be or not to be transparent
under wear and tear.
I try to dress her up in peach lamé,
in sequins—never works.

Eventually Bare Truth emerges
from the bubble bath of babble;
I've listened closely, placed
her glam and glitter in the Goodwill bag,
consigned it to persons
who would still dress up Mis-Truth.

Testifying

"And Truth will set you free?"
A magic key in her apron pocket?
Just ask Joan of Arc, Anita Hill, or Hera.
A key to pearly gates or prison doors?
Not likely. But sometimes
Truth will share her key to cages we have
built around ourselves.
The jury's out.

Honestly?

Constance Truth is not an easy friend.
She never feels she has to compromise.
Her brother Half Truth cannot comprehend

her constant righteousness. He would addend
all blanks not filled, with rumor—criticize
his sibling Truth. "She's not an easy friend,

"my sister. As for me, I must defend
myself if caught in fibs, in jams, in lies."
Blind brother Half Truth does not comprehend.

We really do not need to know or mend
the whole Truth family when we realize
on most days Connie Truth's a better friend

when only known in part. Why can't she bend?
He is mostly right, but in her eyes
it's Half Truth that she cannot comprehend.

Knowing, while it pays a dividend,
makes no one richer; it can ostracize
the one who's right. This, Half does comprehend,
but Connie Truth can live without a friend.

After Election Day, 2012

I shiver
when I come around the corner,
and witness
on a pole held high
a poster
of our re-elected
President
Obama inked
with a Hitler-like mustache.
Slashed across his chest:
Impeach him Now!

Two young men in suits
hold the sign,
offer leaflets
below the flag
of the US Post Office.

I will write a letter
to the *Transcript.*

Friends warn
You must not send this letter.

Vengeance, Saith the Crowd
Boston, April 15-19, 2013

Tamerlan, now dead, had planned the mayhem:
Pressure-cooker recipe, explosives severing arms
and legs. His younger brother ran him over twice,
fleeing in the SUV they heisted. Abandoning all
he fled down darkened alleys to a backyard boat—
refuge on the *Slip Away* in Watertown.
He could not slip away, curled in his pool of blood
and shit until cop bullets peppered half the hull.

Two weeks later, turmoil on the street
of a Worcester Funeral Parlor. People waving signs
and shouting, *We don't owe him nothin'.*
Send him back to Chechnya to his mother-fucking mother.
No resting place in Boston, Lowell, nor even Cambridge
where he'd lived— the city manager asserts
"His body would disturb the peace."

And so it was, even for Hector, vanquished in the Trojan War.
Achilles dragged the body behind his chariot for days.
And so it was for Metacomet slain to end King Philip's War—
body cut in pieces, head was mounted on a pike
in Plymouth where it stayed for twenty years.

Time to Reboot

Today our phone-booth privacy is gone.
A cell-phone buzz in my pocket or my purse
disrupts all train of thought. We don't converse
at meals or with the check-out clerk. Withdrawn,
engaged to texting (almost married), led
down aisles in earbud faux reality,
our isolation grows in each locality—
eye contact hurried, harried.
                              Now, instead,
imagine mockingbirds on evening walks;
listen as the breeze disturbs the willow. Hear
green peepers trading news in swampy reeds.
Turn off technology to notice hawks.
Reboot your brain with silence—let it clear.
Study the complexity of weeds.

Obituary

Penny Palmer-Cursive passed this week at 113.
A descendant of the celebrated Cursive clan, and
robust until 1983, her decline has since been steady.

In childhood a beauty, she stopped hearts
with elegant E's, consorted with decorative ZZZ's,
but ultimately was replaced by Cap Block Printing.

Famous for her professional career
copying documents, best works include
The Bill of Rights, The Constitution.

Preceded in death by her husband Dr. Slide W. Rule.
Her current companion, Long Division, is not well.
Ms. Cursive is survived by a grandson R.U. Texting,

and her estranged and touchy son, Bill Typing.
Her grandchild Wendy Word-Processing
drowned a year ago keyboarding south of Sausalito.

Cursive also leaves a Russian uncle, Cyrillic.
Her stepsister, Calligraphy, suffering
delusions, is now in State Hospital.

A celebration of Penny's life will be held
at the Library of Congress, with calling hours.
In lieu of flowers, her family asks

remembrances be placed on Instagram or
at *www.endCursive.edu.*
At the request of her kin, please

omit handwritten notes.

Pearl Street on Saturday Night
Boulder, Colorado

White tents, a settlement of artisans selling
turquoise bracelets, silk-screened orange mats;
a unicycle rider jumping fire, acrobats.

Salt, the chichi eatery wafts garlic, while outside,
frozen yogurt drips from lips to pavement.
Sweaty minglers, bumping shoulders, egos.

Boys cruise with wheels on the heels of their Nikes. Parade
of tank tops, skirts that barely cover butts, bandanas, bling.
Violin cases cry for coins at every corner:

Banjo janglers, fiddler fanglers, djembe drummers.
A tattooed singer—curly chest hair, knee-torn jeans—
Beer-bellied bruiser with a big blue bass,

sultry lady painted on its back. He strums that girl—
the crowd boogies—as he spins that girl,
leans her to her side, presses her neck, and croons.

Trail Head

Another birthday, just another year.
At twenty I have world enough and time.
My path looks straight, so what could interfere?

At thirty I am into my career
when willing children join the tree-lined climb.
My birthday jolts into another year.

At forty, illness stuns: my parents' cracked veneer
as death accompanies driving rain, mud, slime.
A rocky path—crevasses interfere.

Fifty! Offspring independent. Sphere
of lavender fields, sunflowers, poets' prime
repeating birthday marks another year.

Weddings, first grandchild at sixty. Now near
tree line, I dip in rainbows—summertime.
The summit's next—no brush to interfere.

At seventy? The rock face drop's severe.
Still steeped in effort, I hear midnight's chime.
This decade starts with just another year.
God knows what slithers in to interfere.

Easvesdropping at my 50th Reunion
after a reading of the names of the deceased

Laurie,
lapsed-Methodist, teeters on 7-inch, red Gucci heels,
twirls her artfully streaked shoulder-length hair,
fluffs her black and gold neck scarf, and pronounces:
> *I've been thinking of life and death lately*
> *and recently changed my mind.*
> *Now I think when the lights go out . . .*
(she leans closer, hoarse whisper)
> *the lights go out . . . done.*

Chrissy,
one of the "popular girls," now a Realtor
with leathery wrinkles around her pursed mouth.
White hair, a helmet of spray, she caresses
her seventeenth glass of merlot:
> *Seriously? I have to say*
> *when the lights go out*
> *there's a lot goin' on in the dark.*

Hershel,
wrinkled brown slacks, shirt untucked, limbs akimbo,
gray eyes peeking out under bushy white brows.
A rabbi in lower Manhattan for 45 years, he intones:
> *It often takes time for pupils*
> *to adjust before seeing*
> *something in darkness.*

On Reading Robert Wrigley's 16 Tips, Quips & Pontifications the Week after my 50th Reunion

I truly have tried to live alliteratively.
Count syllables, watch my right margins,
stitch and unstitch decades of decasyllabic lines.
When I don't know what comes next,
I pull down something that's already there.

Every line has a life of its own.
Every life has a line of its own.
Robb Wiggins, a line-giver for sure, my crush
in seventh grade. Firm handshake. Lawyer. Wall Street
money. Lives in Larchmont. Could that be *his* hair?

There used to be prose poems I loved,
but I, like Wrigley, have no impulse now to write one.
Nor to spend another evening sharing
shrimp bites, faded photos, looks.
I've written books. Sound drives my poems,

a convertible Gatsby sound, like jazz at the end.
Surprisingly, Mike Cusa's fingers, tapping foot, bald head
know how to swing it on a lobby babygrand. Cusa,
in the lower grades, used to sport a wave of jet-black hair.
In poetry nothing is used up, or ever gone.

The list is read: twenty-nine dead. But here
we stand (except Marie who has a cane)
to tell what we have done these 50 years.
There are no cliques, no snubs, no lies.
There are no rules. We ate them all.

With Appreciation

For their advice and encouragement, special thanks to
Linda Salisbury
Frances McCormick
Patricia Callan
Jane Gossard
Joan Kimball
Barbara Lydecker Crane
Sonia Wallenberg
Don Miller
and always Rhina Espaillat

About the Author

Nancy Bailey Miller has published five books of poems. Her poetry has appeared in many printed and on-line journals including *Rattapallax, Quill & Parchment, Blue Unicorn, Poetry Porch,* and *Lighten Up Online.* Anthologized in the *Powow River Anthology* and *Merrimack Literary Review,* her work most recently appeared in *The Crafty Poet, A Portable Workshop,* and was chosen *Poem of the Moment* by the masspoetry.org website for July 6, 2015.

A member of the Powow River Poets in Newburyport, Bartlet Street Poets of Andover, and The Quartet Poets in Burlington, Nancy has also attended writing workshops at Frost Place in Franconia, New Hampshire, Fine Arts Work Center in Provincetown, Massachusetts, Omega Institute in Rhinebeck, New York, as well as the University of New Mexico in Taos. She has worked with Sharon Olds, Liz Rosenberg, Martín Espada, and others.

Retired from Phillips Academy Andover, Bailey Miller taught writing in the Summer Session there for ten years. A sailor on her dad's Town Class boat at age ten, and for many years racing on various sailboats out of Marblehead Harbor, Nancy is now regular racing crew on her husband's PHRF boat, *Feather II.*

Notes

p.15 "Raw Water and Fresh"
Raw water on a boat is saltwater used to cool the engine, flush the heads, etc. The head is the toilet on a boat.

p.18 "Eerste Helmersstraat"
A residential street in Amsterdam not far from Vondel Park. The Leideseplein is a busy square nearby where one can buy tickets for the "Hop-on-Hop-off" canal boat ride.

p.19 "Zip Line in Chile with Strangers"
This takes place at an eco-resort at Huilo Huilo, Chile, many hours south of Santiago. *Spanish translation: el bosque = woods, ¿Entiende usted? = Do you understand? ¿Lista? = Ready? ¡Me voy! = Here I go!*

p.20 "Rubén's Story"
On a bus to Cuzco our Peruvian tour guide, Rubén Aragón, told us this story about his family. He was also the inspiration for "Outside the Textile Shop." *Spanish translation: piscina = swimming pool, ¡Que lástima!=What a shame!*

p.24 "Wrong Direction"
On a bike trip in Costa Brava, Spain. *Spanish translation: El pueblo de Bisbal? Donde está? = The town of Bisbal? Where is it?*

p.26 "Why Jack Ewing Got into Eco-tourism"
Hacienda Baru encompasses 813 acres of what now is National
Wildlife Refuge on the Pacific coastline in Costa Rica, an area Jack
Ewing has spent a lifetime reforesting so that monkeys, pumas and
other indigenous creatures can follow their migratory patterns in
Central America.

p.31 "Flight 370"
Malaysian Airlines Flight 370 disappeared on March 8, 2014, after
departing from Kuala Lumpur for Beijing with 239 passengers and
crew members on board. Malaysia's prime minister stated that the
aircraft's flight ended somewhere in the Indian Ocean, but no
further explanation has been given. The incident remains under
investigation.

Afterwords

Ashes

My parents opted for the Florida Gulf.
Mother: in a pink Minton teapot
drifting, slipping into sand shifting
below the Peace River.
Father: in a Folger's can
bobbing with dolphins, refusing to sink.

For now, my spouse chooses the ocean,
but for me . . . I'm thinking of earth.
After all my life's roaming and turbulence,
I envision a village of mossy stones,
home to a hamlet of sparrow-filled maples.
I want to be planted, stay put.

www.ingramcontent.com/pod-product-compliance
Lightning Source LLC
LaVergne TN
LVHW091210080426
835509LV00006B/920